Presentations

20 MINUTE MANAGER SERIES

Get up to speed fast on essential business skills. Whether you're looking for a crash course or a brief refresher, you'll find just what you need in HBR's 20-Minute Manager series—foundational reading for ambitious professionals and aspiring executives. Each book is a concise, practical primer, so you'll have time to brush up on a variety of key management topics.

Advice you can quickly read and apply, from the most trusted source in business.

Titles include:

Creating Business Plans

Delegating Work

Finance Basics

Managing Projects

Managing Time

Managing Up

Presentations

Running Meetings

2⊘ MINUTE MANAGER SERIES

Presentations

Sharpen your message
Persuade your audience
Gauge your impact

HARVARD BUSINESS REVIEW PRESS

Boston, Massachusetts

Copyright 2014 Harvard Business School Publishing Corporation

All rights reserved
Printed in the United States of America
10 9 8 7 6 5 4 3 2 1

The web addresses referenced in this book were live and correct at
the time of the book's publication but may be subject to change.

Library of Congress Cataloging-in-Publication Data

Presentations.
       pages cm
    ISBN 978-1-62527-086-3 (alk. paper)
1. Business presentations.
    HF5718.22 P74 2014
    658.4'52—dc23

2013024774

Preview

It takes more than personality and PowerPoint to give an effective presentation. But you can learn how, whether you're presenting for the first time or you just need a refresher. This book walks you through the basic steps:

- Articulating a clear message.

- Tailoring it to your audience.

- Organizing your content.

- Gathering relevant, persuasive data.

- Choosing the right tools and visual aids.

- Rehearsing and getting feedback.

- Delivering your talk with clarity and confidence.

- Fielding questions and following up.

- Making improvements for next time.

Contents

The Key to Presenting   1

Why Give a Presentation?   5

Define Your Goal   9

Your broad objective   11

Your desired outcomes   12

Your measurement of success   14

Know Your Audience   15

Craft Your Message   23

Step 1: Define your core message   26

Step 2: Identify relevant arguments and data   27

Step 3: Organize the content   28

Contents

Identify Your Resources   35

What's your venue like?   *37*

How much time will you have?   *38*

What equipment will you use?   *39*

Plan the Visuals   41

Choosing the appropriate media   *44*

Creating effective visuals   *44*

Practice Your Delivery   49

Rehearsing your content   *51*

Preparing yourself mentally   *54*

Deliver Your Presentation   57

Keeping your audience engaged   *60*

Being flexible   *61*

Manage the Response   65

Timing the Q&A   *67*

Preparing for tough questions   *68*

Outlining next steps   *70*

Debrief Your Presentation   73

Critiquing your content   75

Analyzing your performance   76

Asking colleagues for feedback   77

Follow Up with the Audience   79

Learn More   *83*

Sources   *93*

Index   *95*

Presentations

The Key to
Presenting

The Key to Presenting

You have a message to communicate, and you've decided to give a presentation. You'll need to do some work to win people over to your way of thinking. But that's definitely not out of reach, even if you don't consider yourself a naturally gifted public speaker.

No matter what form your presentation takes—whether it's a status report, a product demonstration, a sales pitch, or a strategy rollout—the key to presenting effectively is to know your goals, your audience, and yourself. That core idea informs all the principles in this book.

Let's get right to them.

Why Give a Presentation?

Why Give a Presentation?

I f you're planning to present to a business audience, you probably want to inform, persuade, or sell. This may entail:

- Explaining new data.

- Soliciting ideas or feedback to build consensus.

- Asking people to take action.

- Seeking help solving a problem.

- Getting buy-in on an initiative.

Are you trying to do one of those things or something else? Write down your purpose in a phrase as short as the ones listed above.

Now look at what you wrote and ask whether you even need to give a presentation. Is that the best way to get the job done?

For example, if the number of people you need to reach is quite small, perhaps a quick face-to-face chat with each of them would be more efficient. If the audience is larger but the message is simple and you don't need feedback, an e-mail might suffice.

Sometimes, of course, those forms of communication are inadequate and it's clear you'll need to give a presentation. If that's the case, you're ready to start working on yours. Hold on to that purpose phrase you wrote down a moment ago; you'll need it.

Define
Your Goal

Define Your Goal

An effective presentation begins with focused thinking. You'll need to figure out your primary aim, which usually involves getting people to understand something or take action.

Your broad objective

Go back to that short phrase you wrote down earlier—turn it into a crisp sentence that states your goal. Begin with "I want," and include your audience. Here are some examples:

- "I want to inform my department about the new process for proposing new product ideas."

- "I want my colleagues to help brainstorm ideas for the project we're about to start."

- "I want to show people how well my team's new system works."

- "I want to get other managers to sign on to a set of recommendations I've developed for our top executives."

- "I want to give people in my group the tools they need to reach their targets this quarter."

Your broad objective may be nothing like those, but state it just as succinctly. Anyone should be able to understand it without reading it twice.

Your desired outcomes

Now it's time to get specific, not about what your presentation will include (that comes later) but about what results you want. Take, for example, this objective from the preceding list:

> "I want to show people how well my team's new system works."

You don't just want attendees to walk away impressed with the system. You seek outcomes. What are they? Maybe you need people to identify ways they can use the system in their daily work or to take the first step toward implementation within one week. Or maybe you'd like them to troubleshoot obstacles and report back to you with their findings within 10 days.

Whatever your desired outcomes, write them down in a list. There's no magic number, but be realistic; fewer items are usually better. That way, you'll tighten your focus and avoid setting your own and your audience's expectations too high.

Your measurement of success

With your broad objective and desired outcomes in hand, identify how you will measure whether you've met your goals.

Do you expect to leave the presentation with ideas that audience members generated? Do you want attendees to complete a set of tasks by a certain deadline? Are you trying to measure "soft" data, such as enthusiasm and buy-in? How will you gauge those?

Keep the metrics simple and easy to assess, accounting for what your audience can realistically produce. If you're looking for feedback, you might ask people to complete a brief form or online survey. If deliverables are part of the mix, provide a handout that lists those items—something physical that audience members can carry away with them and that you can easily send to people who missed the presentation.

Know Your Audience

Know Your Audience

T he better you understand your audience's goals and concerns, the more likely you are to achieve your objective and your desired outcomes. And the better able you will be to measure those successes.

The audience, not the presenter, is the heart of any presentation. To figure out what makes it tick, answer these questions:

1. *How big will the group be? Who will be absent?* Are you expecting 5, 15, or 50 people? The size of the audience affects the type of presentation you'll give and the resources you'll need (see "Identify Your Resources" later

in this book). Keep track of which people can't attend. Absent stakeholders are stakeholders nonetheless; you'll want to follow up with them afterward.

2. *What roles do your audience members perform in the organization? To whom are they accountable?* Having a basic understanding of their responsibilities will help you engage them. Consider why your message matters to them and how you can make their lives easier. You'll highlight those things when you present.

3. *What does the audience already know? What do people need to know?* Don't state the obvious, but give people enough background information to understand what you're saying and how it affects them.

4. *What are people likely to assume? Which of those assumptions are correct and which incorrect?* Anticipating your audience's assump-

tions helps you make better choices about how to present your content. If there's a misperception you need to correct, this might be the time to do it—gently. For example, if your audience believes that the new system you're proposing will take too much time and effort to learn, clearly explain how you'll help ease the transition with training sessions and extra technical support.

5. *How well does the audience know you?* If you don't already have strong relationships with the people in the room, you'll need to establish a rapport with them early on. For instance, you might open with an amusing anecdote about your own struggles with the old system you'd like to replace. Show that you share the group's frustrations with the way things are.

6. *Will some attendees' goals conflict with others'?* If so, acknowledge that up front and explain how what you have to offer may help.

7. *What types of presentations are your audience members accustomed to?* Think about what's likely to get their attention, given what's worked in the past (data, demonstrations, personal stories). If you're doing something that's new to them, find ways to make them comfortable with it. Talking to a group of number crunchers? Open with a relevant story to give your presentation greater personal meaning, but make it one that they can relate to.

8. *Is someone requiring them to be there? Is that person you?* This will affect how receptive people are to your message. You may need to overcome apathy or even hostility.

9. *Will you or someone else hold them accountable for what happens during or after the presentation?* Consult with the attendees' managers about the feedback or deliverables you'll be soliciting, to make sure your goals align with theirs.

Not every question here will be relevant to your presentation. And, clearly, other pertinent considerations exist. The point is not to write up answers to a bunch of questions in a handy book. It's to reflect on the human context in which you will deliver your message so you can tailor it to suit your audience's challenges and goals.

Anticipating the needs and concerns of your audience helps you calibrate your mind-set as you prepare and execute your presentation. Take the old adage about putting yourself in others' shoes to the next level: *Put yourself inside their heads and behind their eyes. Imagine yourself sitting there witnessing what you have to say.*

Did you do that? *Really* do that? OK, now you're ready to craft your message.

Craft Your Message

Craft Your Message

Many presenters mistakenly assume that a great idea will speak for itself, as long as it comes in an appealing package. Packaging matters, no doubt, but your audience needs much more than that. Guide people through your logic, facts, and examples, but without bogging them down in details that don't pertain to them. You want them to arrive where you are and, ideally, enjoy getting there. So chart a clear path by following three basic steps.

Step 1: Define your core message

What main point do you want people to remember when they walk away from the presentation? That's your core message. As with the phrase stating your purpose for presenting, it should be short and sweet. But test your assumptions: Have you really chosen the most critical message to articulate? Does it jibe with your objective and desired outcomes (see "Define Your Goal" earlier in this book)? Make sure your answer to both questions is a resounding yes.

Every part of your presentation should advance the message you select. Does that mean you need to keep repeating it? Of course not. But almost anything you say or show that doesn't support your main point may weaken it and undercut your goals. So keep a tight focus here. It will help you choose the right supporting material in Step 2.

Step 2: Identify relevant arguments and data

Every good presentation makes a case. And a strong case needs support.

Back up each assertion with well-chosen facts and data. Statements made without evidence are merely opinions, and opinions alone don't move an audience. Give people reasons to share your views or adopt a course of action.

Include only those facts and data that will persuade. Extraneous details distract listeners from what you want them to hear, process, and remember. If you're not sure about the value of a point, leave it out.

Excluding the extraneous doesn't mean focusing only on cold, hard data. It's also important to connect emotionally. Be explicit about why your audience should care about your message. Tap into the anger or pain wrought by the status quo.

After you've gathered material for your argument, step back and reflect:

- Will everyone in your audience be able to follow you? Or will you need to briefly define terms or provide a little more background to bring some people up to speed?

- Will your supporting content persuade your audience? What else might you need to make your case?

- Are you showing people why what you're saying should matter to them?

- Are you making their journey engaging?

Step 3: Organize the content

A well-organized presentation makes it easier for the audience to listen and for you to achieve your goals.

Logically sequence your argument so that people can follow it from one point to the next.

Let's return to the example discussed earlier: If you're proposing a new system, first briefly explain why the old one has to go and how the new one solves those problems. Then spell out how the new system works and how the audience can start reaping its benefits.

In most cases, a presentation should have four parts: an opening, a description of the need or problem you're addressing, your proposed solution, and a call to action.

The opening

Use a hook—a comment, relevant story, statement, or example—to get your audience's attention. Look for ways to engage attendees right away: For instance, you might ask for a show of hands in response to a provocative question that sets up your topic.

In addition to establishing a rapport, a strong opening also:

- Defines the purpose of your presentation.

- Highlights what's in it for the audience.

- Confirms your credibility.

- Previews the main points very briefly.

The need or problem

Keep this part of your presentation tight and focused so you'll have plenty of time to propose your solution.

An effective statement of the need or problem:

- Spells out the main challenge you want to address with the audience's help.

- Shows how that issue directly affects the audience.

- Has a sense of urgency.

- Reflects thoughtful input from others—through employee surveys, for example.

- Incorporates relevant arguments, examples, and supporting material that sustain interest without distracting from the point.

The solution

Now it's time to say how you think the problem should be solved or the need satisfied. You'll want to:

- Help audience members visualize the benefits of your solution.

- Phrase your solution in terms of their needs.

- Use a story, when possible, to illustrate the solution.

- Involve the audience in developing a path forward.

- Make sure the strength of your solution matches the challenge.

ASKING THE AUDIENCE FOR INPUT

Figure out in advance when you'll ask people for input during your presentation. You may simply want to ensure they're with you as you lay out your argument, but you also may wish to draw on their knowledge to support your message.

Empty questions aimed at the whole sweep of the room—"Is everybody following?"—generally don't work. Most polite people will simply nod. Instead, directly address individuals: "Does that seem like the biggest problem with customer satisfaction, Maria, given your front-line perspective?"

Asking audience members what they think is a great way to heed the pleasure principle. When people feel their voices and ideas are being heard, they're happy and more likely to open their minds to what they're hearing from you.

Call to action

A good wrap-up has a strong call to action. These are the key ingredients:

- Reiterate the challenge and your solution.

- Recommend specific action.

- Obtain commitment or buy-in.

- Agree on assignments if appropriate.

- Explain what you'll be doing to follow up after the presentation.

Identify Your Resources

Identify Your Resources

Know exactly what resources you'll have at your disposal the day you present so you can plan to make the most of them. These include the physical space you'll be in, the amount of time you'll get, and the equipment you'll have in the room.

What's your venue like?

If possible, visit the venue and scope out any limitations. Note where you'll be standing and how far away the most remote audience member will be. Decide whether you'll need a microphone to be heard. Also assess the seating: People who have to stand through a presentation are more likely to leave early than those who have a chair.

How much time will you have?

Pace yourself so you can make your argument comfortably within the window you have. Factor in audience feedback and participation when you budget your time. Also think about the time available to you after the presentation is over—for informal chats, feedback surveys, collection of deliverables, return visits, and so on.

Often you must fit your presentation into a timetable that someone else develops. For example, you may have 30 minutes to deliver a sales presentation to a buyer. In other instances, you control the timing. The following guidelines are helpful in both situations:

- Speak just long enough to convey your key message clearly and completely.

- It's better to make fewer points and make them well.

- If you don't have time to make a point clear or acceptable to your audience, omit it or save it for another presentation.

- Ending early is better than not completing the talk or rushing at the end.

- Plan what to skip if your time is cut short.

What equipment will you use?

If a particular tool enhances your content, make sure you can use it competently. Delays that occur because you can't work the equipment will annoy the audience and may throw you off your game.

The next chapter of this book is about planning your visual aids. But before you turn to that, you'll need to know what tools you'll have handy: paper, whiteboards, projectors, a laser pointer, video conferencing, or other possibilities. Catalog what's available, and secure anything extra that you need.

Also check that any network passwords you'll need to access files, an internet connection, or other software and devices are up-to-date. Test them out before the presentation to make sure log-ins will be seamless.

Plan the Visuals

Plan the Visuals

The visuals are often what stick with people well after a presentation ends. Consider these research findings:

- People learn 75% of what they know visually, 13% through hearing, and 12% through smell.

- A picture is three times as effective in conveying information as words alone.

- Words and pictures together are six times as effective as words alone.

So use visual aids to help your audience stay engaged, remember facts, and understand ideas, relationships, or physical layouts. You can also use them as cues that you're moving to a new topic. Remember, however, that when people are looking at a visual, they're not looking at you. That's why it's important to create visuals that they can process quickly.

Choosing the appropriate media

You have many choices for your visuals, including PowerPoint, video, and paper handouts. When selecting your media, consider flexibility, cost, appropriateness for your presentation, and your comfort level with the format or technology. If you use handouts, avoid distributing them during the presentation. It detracts from what you're saying.

Creating effective visuals

Not all visuals enhance a presentation. Put together a thick deck of boring slides, for example, and you'll inflict "death by PowerPoint"—something you've probably experienced as an audience member.

Steer clear of the following traps, which will frustrate your audience or even put people to sleep:

- Having too many slides.

- Using complex, confusing visuals, such as flow charts with lots of boxes, arrows, feedback loops, and text.

- Packing your visuals border-to-border with dense text or too many images.

- Simply reading the text in your visuals aloud.

To make your visuals more compelling, keep them simple. Use:

- Graphics, icons, and symbols to reinforce concepts.

- Key words, not full sentences.

- Only one concept and no more than six lines of text per slide or page.

- Only three to six ideas on each flip chart or whiteboard display.

- Color where possible, but not excessively.

- Pictures where feasible.

- Bullets, not numbers, for nonsequential items.

- All-uppercase letters only for titles or acronyms.

See what a difference it makes when you clear away the visual clutter:

Before

We follow the same basic process every time

- We start with the invention. We take early stage ideas and turn them into demos—not technical demos but conceptual ones, like the rough version of Flare you saw.

- Then our team takes this seed of an idea to customers, in conferences and forums, to get feedback that helps us shape it into something even more useful.

- We improve it and build a prototype that we give to a set of early adopters, who use it and give us more feedback.

- Eventually, after a few quick cycles of this process, we standardize the product features.

- Only then is it ready to go out to our larger group of customers, like the finished version of Flare you saw.

After

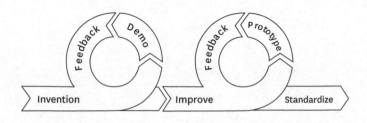

Source: Nancy Duarte, *HBR Guide to Persuasive Presentations* (Boston: Harvard Business Review Press, 2012).

Now that you've planned your presentation, it's time to practice it.

Practice
Your Delivery

Practice Your Delivery

I t feels great when you've finished creating a presentation. Indeed, many presenters feel so satisfied that they do nothing else until it's time to speak. But to prepare thoroughly, you must also rehearse what you're going to say and get yourself ready mentally so you're both polished and relaxed.

Rehearsing your content

It's tough to identify all the holes, dull spots, and excessive details in your presentation just by reviewing your notes and slides. You need to assess how your presentation will look and sound to other people.

The best way to do that is to practice before a test audience. If you can, rehearse in front of a group of colleagues or friends. Try to include people who are similar to your real audience in terms of their roles, assumptions, perspectives, and expertise (see "Know Your Audience" earlier in this book). Interact with the test audience as you would with your actual audience.

Of course, time and other constraints may not permit you to rehearse with a live group. In that case, play back an audio or video recording of yourself: You'll find flaws you wouldn't have discovered otherwise. Even practicing aloud in front of a mirror gives you the chance to hear your own voice and see how you're coming across—though it's hard to deliver your talk and assess yourself at the same time, so it's no substitute for live feedback or a recording.

Other tips to remember as you rehearse:

- Practice with the equipment you're planning to use.

- Use visual aids to reinforce your message, not to speak for you.

- Know your content well so you won't have your nose in your notes, but don't script yourself word for word—it'll sound memorized.

- Rehearse the entire presentation to see how it all hangs together.

- Use an expressive, conversational voice.

- Avoid jargon and other terms your audience may not know.

- Articulate responses to questions that people are likely to ask you. Focus on your tone.

- Ask yourself, "What's the worst that can happen during the presentation?" Prepare for that possibility by mapping out how you'll move past it.

- Practice in the same room where you'll present, if that venue is available.

Preparing yourself mentally

Rehearsing your talk is one thing; putting yourself in the right state of mind before the curtain opens is another—and just as important. To win the mental game, try these techniques right before the presentation:

- Visualize yourself giving a successful presentation.

- Repeat positive statements to yourself, such as "I am relaxed and ready."

- Use deep-breathing and tension-relieving exercises to reduce stress.

- Wear clothing that makes you feel comfortable, confident, and professional.

- Accept nervousness as natural. Don't try to counteract it with food, caffeine, drugs, or alcohol.

- Interact with audience members as they come into the room.

Deliver Your Presentation

Deliver Your Presentation

Once you're in the room with your audience, focus on engaging people and projecting confidence. Here are some suggestions that will help:

- Retain the expressive, conversational tone you practiced in your rehearsal.

- Speak at a moderate pace. You'll sound nervous if you go too fast; you'll bore people if you go too slowly.

- Make sure everyone can hear you. If you have a microphone and sound system, test its effectiveness before you begin.

- Avoid watering down what you say with "kind of" and "sort of."

- Make eye contact with audience members.

- Watch the audience for nonverbal cues, and use your facial expressions to convey interest in people's reactions.

- Take a breath now and then. It helps you relax and reduces filler language such as "um" and "er."

Keeping your audience engaged

You'll probably confront one or more difficult audience members: the tuned out, the overloaded, or the just plain grumpy. Inattentive people often cross their legs, fidget in their seats, or look around the room more than usual. Here are some proven techniques for grabbing their attention:

- Change what you're doing—pause, for example, or alter your tone of voice.

- Survey the audience: "Just out of curiosity, how many of you believe that our customers are satisfied with our current returns policy? Let's see a show of hands."

- Add humor if appropriate. Audience members welcome a little comic relief.

- Provide analogies and vivid examples.

- Introduce personal stories.

- Keep returning to how your message affects the audience: "Here's what that last point means for you and your team."

Being flexible

Even the most well-planned, meticulously rehearsed presentation is a dynamic event. Rarely does everything go by the book. Technical difficulties may arise, circumstances affecting your content may change right before you speak, and audience reactions may take an unexpected turn. You can anticipate some wrinkles, as discussed in "Know Your Audience" earlier in this book. But you must be willing to embrace unforeseen developments and to remain flexible in the face of them.

A presenter who refuses to deviate from his or her plan risks being perceived as having a tin ear, a thick skull, or, worst of all, a flawed message. Treat unexpected developments as opportunities, not threats. Don't allow them to derail you from your core message, but don't just barrel ahead without addressing them, either.

This is especially important when an audience member throws you a curveball question or comment (see the next chapter, "Manage the Response"). If someone asks for more evidence on a peripheral point, for instance, view that as a chance to make an even stronger case. If you have more data in your pocket, share what you've got or offer to do extra research after the presentation.

When technical or logistical problems arise, brush them off with good humor. A joke in the face of a glitch is a testament to your confidence and level of preparation, and it shows that your message is more important than the medium.

Manage the
Response

Manage the Response

Some people feel that a presentation that generates no questions is a success. But if your listeners are engaged, they are very likely to have questions. Embracing those inquiries can allow you to offer greater detail in areas that matter to your audience.

Timing the Q&A

Many speakers take questions after they present. This allows them to complete the talk within a specified time and to ensure the audience has the whole picture. If you choose that approach:

- Make your transition to the Q&A session clear.

- Tell the audience how much time is left for Q&A.

- Maintain control of the Q&A session by repeating each question and giving the answer to the whole group, not only to the questioner.

You may decide to take questions throughout the presentation or ask for reactions and ideas along the way to keep people engaged. In your notes, identify places where you'd like audience feedback so you won't forget to ask for it. Tell people explicitly why you're pausing. That will help them focus their questions and comments. Keep your own questions and responses brief so that the presentation stays on track.

Preparing for tough questions

Suppose you're presenting your unit's new strategic plan to a group of anxious managers and employees.

Or the CEO has asked you to go to each regional office to explain upcoming layoffs.

What do these situations have in common? The great potential for resistance. Here's how to handle it:

1. *Anticipate tough questions.* Before you present, write down whatever objections you think may come up and brainstorm how you'll respond. Run your responses by a trusted colleague to make sure you'll give those objections a fair hearing.

2. *Be gracious, not defensive.* Show curiosity and enthusiasm in both the tone and content of your responses. Replies such as "That's a great question, and here's why . . ." make it clear that you have already thought about things from the audience's perspective. Be open to exploring options you hadn't considered, and the people raising them will be more likely to hear you out, too.

3. *Don't try to be all things to everyone.* If people raise questions that go beyond the scope of your presentation, don't hesitate to say so. They'll understand that you had to draw a line somewhere.

4. *Answer questions honestly.* When you know the answer, articulate it clearly and briefly. When you don't know it, admit that. Either direct the questioner to another source or offer to do some digging yourself. Write down questions you can't address on the spot to demonstrate your commitment to answering them.

Outlining next steps

Even if the questions you get aren't especially tough, show that your message has a life beyond the presentation. For instance:

- Specify how—and to whom--audience members should give their feedback about the presentation.

- Explain how deliverables, if any, should be transmitted to you or others (see "Define Your Goal" earlier in this book).

- Offer whatever support you can to help people put your ideas into action.

- If a follow-up presentation or other event is planned, provide whatever relevant details you have.

- Emphasize your genuine interest in continuing the conversation if there's more to discuss.

- When you're sharing your contact information, be sure of your ability to respond and promise to do just that.

- If feasible, talk to attendees as they leave the room. Don't allow one or two people to

monopolize your time so that others feel
snubbed.

Now that the presentation itself is finished, it's
time to debrief what happened and to measure your
success.

Debrief Your Presentation

Debrief Your Presentation

You wrapped up your presentation by outlining next steps for the audience. Of course, you'll follow through on your end of those commitments (see the next chapter, "Follow Up with the Audience"). But you also have an obligation to honestly assess the talk you just gave and to sharpen your skills before your next one.

Critiquing your content

No matter how well you've planned your presentation, the act of delivering it will often expose flaws, gaps, or other shortcomings, even if you're a polished presenter.

You may discover small glitches, such as a slide that could not be read from the back of the room, or bigger ones, like a missing step in a process you outlined. Make a list of those flaws as soon as possible— no more than an hour or two after your presentation ends, if that's feasible. Incorporate the changes into your slides and other master files within a few days. Trying to reconstruct and correct the problems weeks or months later almost always yields worse results, if you remember to fix the mistakes at all.

Analyzing your performance

Problems with delivery run the gamut. You can easily identify minor ones, such as weak opening remarks and awkward attempts at humor, the moment they happen. Just look at the audience's reaction: Are people nodding? Or is everyone sitting dead still? Watching a video recording of the event will also help you see trouble spots. Think of specific fixes for next time, and write them down.

If you ran into technical problems, they may have thrown your whole talk off track, but those, too, are relatively simple to fix. Perhaps you really didn't know how to use the projector, and that slowed you down or made you fumble. Learn how to use it for next time. Enlist an assistant if appropriate.

Chronic issues, such as your general comfort level and skill in delivery, require more work. If you felt very nervous the entire time (not just during the first few minutes) or if you found yourself clinging to notes or stammering despite having rehearsed thoroughly, you may need some coaching.

Asking colleagues for feedback

If trusted coworkers were in the audience, tap them for advice on how to improve your presentation and on how to become a better presenter. Set up one-on-one meetings to receive that feedback. A quick "How did I do?" in the corridor is likely to generate a polite, perhaps less than honest, response, particularly if other people are within earshot. Your meetings with your colleagues should be brief and informal, but don't be afraid to ask for people's frank reactions to both the content and the delivery of your presentation.

It takes a long time to master presentation skills. But if you continuously work to improve, your presentations will become more and more effective, and your standing with your audiences will rise.

Follow Up with the Audience

Follow Up with the Audience

Your presentation is finished, and you've evaluated how it went. You can relax now, but not for too long. Even the most well-articulated ideas can evaporate into thin air if you don't take concrete steps to make sure they're implemented.

Of course, you should keep the promises you made during the presentation ("I'll send those tables to you, Beth") and correct any errors that came to light. You will certainly want to follow up on explicit directives you've given, such as asking the audience to report back to you about a key item within a specified time frame. But those are just the essentials. Other gestures can also make a big difference. These include:

- Sending thank-you notes to key attendees.

- E-mailing the entire audience to briefly re-inforce your takeaway message and to get your address in their in-boxes.

- Making yourself available for questions that occur to people after the presentation.

- Booking "next steps" meetings to ensure that your implementation plan proceeds efficiently.

- Giving the same or a similar presentation to another group that needs to hear your message.

Whatever follow-up techniques you choose, re-member that a presentation is not an isolated event. It fits into a larger context that you share with your audience. If you want to persuade people for the long term, not just for the brief period when you stand in front of them, let them know that you see and under-stand the big picture. They'll be more likely to take action if you do.

Learn More

Books

Duarte, Nancy. *HBR Guide to Persuasive Presentations*. Boston: Harvard Business Review Press, 2012.

Terrified of speaking in front of a group? Or simply looking to polish your skills? No matter where you are on the spectrum, this guide will take the pain out of presentations by giving you the confidence and tools you need to get results. Written by presentation expert Nancy Duarte, the *HBR Guide to Persuasive Presentations* will help you:

- Win over tough crowds.
- Organize a coherent narrative.
- Create powerful messages and visuals.
- Connect with and engage your audience.
- Show people why your ideas matter to them.
- Strike the right tone, in any situation.

Harvard Business School Publishing. *Harvard Business Essentials: Business Communication*. Boston: Harvard Business School Press, 2003.

With advice and tools for improving a wide array of communication skills—from delivering an effective presentation to drafting proposals to the effective use of e-mail—*Business Communication* helps managers deliver information effectively.

Harvard Business School Publishing. *HBR's 10 Must Reads on Communication*. Boston: Harvard Business Review Press, 2013.

The best leaders know how to communicate clearly and persuasively. How do you stack up? If you read nothing else on communicating effectively, read these 10 articles. We've combed through hundreds of articles in the *Harvard Business Review* archive and selected the most important ones to help you express your ideas with clarity and impact, no matter what the situation. Leading experts such as Deborah Tannen, Jay Conger, and Nick Morgan provide the insights and advice you need to:

- Pitch your brilliant idea—successfully.

- Connect with your audience.

- Establish credibility.

- Inspire others to carry out your vision.

- Adapt to stakeholders' decision-making styles.

- Frame goals around common interests.

- Build consensus and win support.

Morgan, Nick. *Give Your Speech, Change the World: How to Move Your Audience to Action.* Boston: Harvard Business Review Press, 2005.

Do you remember the topic of the last speech you heard? If not, you're not alone. Studies show that audiences remember only 10% to 30% of speech or presentation content.

Given those bleak statistics, why do we give speeches at all? We give them, says communications expert Nick Morgan, because they remain the most powerful way of connecting with audiences since ancient Greek times. But as we've evolved to a more conversational mode of public speaking, thanks to television, we have forgotten much of what the Greeks taught us about the nonverbal aspects of speech giving: the physical connection with audiences that can create an almost palpable emotional bond. Morgan says this "kinesthetic connection" comes from truly listening to your audience, not just with your brain but with your body.

In this book, he draws from more than 20 years as a speech coach and consultant, combining the best of ancient Greek oratory with modern communications research to offer a new, audience-centered approach to public speaking. Through entertaining and insightful examples, Morgan illustrates a three-part process—focusing on content development, rehearsal, and delivery—that will enable readers of all experience levels to give more effective, passion-filled speeches that move audiences to action.

Articles

Denning, Stephen. "Telling Tales." *Harvard Business Review*. May 2004 (product #R0405H).

A carefully chosen story can help the leader of an organization translate an abstract concept into a meaningful mandate for employees. The key is to know which narrative strategies are right for what circumstances. Knowledge management expert Stephen Denning explains that, for optimal effect, form should follow function. Challenging one professional storyteller's view that more is better, Denning points out that it's not always desirable (or practical) to launch into an epic that's jam-packed with complex characters, cleverly placed plot points, an intricate rising action, and a neatly resolved denouement. If the aim is to motivate people to act when they might not be inclined to do so, it's best to take an approach that's light on detail; particulars can bog down listeners and prevent them from focusing on the message.

Drawing on his experiences at the World Bank and observations made elsewhere, the author provides several dos and don'ts for organizational storytellers, along with examples of narratives that get results. Denning also presents seven distinct types of stories, the situations in which they should be told, and tips on how to tell them. Leaders with the strength to push past some initial skepticism about the enterprise of storytelling will find that the creative effort pays off.

Elsbach, Kimberly D. "How to Pitch a Brilliant Idea." *Harvard Business Review*. September 2003 (product #R0309J).

Coming up with creative ideas is easy; selling them to strangers is hard. Entrepreneurs, sales executives, and marketing managers often go to great lengths to demonstrate how their new concepts are practical and profitable, only to be rejected by corporate decision makers who don't seem to understand the value of the ideas. Why does this happen?

Having studied Hollywood executives who assess screenplay pitches, the author says the person on the receiving end—the "catcher"—tends to gauge the pitcher's creativity as well as the proposal itself. An impression of the pitcher's ability to come up with workable ideas can quickly and permanently overshadow the catcher's feelings about an idea's worth. To determine whether these observations apply to business settings beyond Hollywood, the author attended product design, marketing, and venture-capital pitch sessions and conducted interviews with executives responsible for judging new ideas. The results in those environments were similar to her observations in Hollywood, she says.

Catchers subconsciously categorize successful pitchers as *showrunners* (smooth and professional), *artists* (quirky and unpolished), or *neophytes* (inexperienced and naive). The research also reveals that catchers tend to respond well when they believe they are participating in an idea's development. As Oscar-winning writer, director, and producer Oliver Stone puts it, a screenwriter pitching an idea should "pull back and project what he needs onto your idea in order to make the story whole for him."

To become a successful pitcher, portray yourself as one of the three creative types and engage your catchers in the creative process. By finding ways to give your catchers a chance to shine, you sell yourself as a likable collaborator.

Guber, Peter. "Four Truths of the Storyteller." *Harvard Business Review*. December 2007 (product #R0712C).

A well-told story's power to captivate and inspire people has been recognized for thousands of years. Peter Guber is in the business of creating compelling stories: He has headed several entertainment companies—including Sony Pictures, PolyGram, and Columbia Pictures—and produced *Rain Man*, *Batman*, and *The Color Purple*, among many other movies. In this article, he offers a method for effectively exercising that power.

For a story to enrapture its listeners, says Guber, it must be *true to the teller*, embodying his or her deepest values and conveying them with candor; *true to the audience*, delivering on the promise that it will be worth people's time by acknowledging listeners' needs and involving them in the narrative; *true to the moment*, appropriately matching the context—whether it's an address to two thousand customers or a chat with a colleague over drinks—yet flexible enough to allow for improvisation; and *true to the mission*, conveying the teller's passion for the worthy endeavor that the story illustrates and enlisting support for it.

In this article, Guber's advice—distilled not only from his years in the entertainment industry but also from an intense discussion over dinner one evening with storytelling experts from various walks of life—is illustrated with numerous examples of effective storytelling from business and elsewhere. Perhaps the most startling is a colorful anecdote about how Guber's own impromptu use of storytelling, while standing on the deck of a ship in Havana harbor, won Fidel Castro's grudging support for a film project.

Morgan, Nick. "How to Become an Authentic Speaker." *Harvard Business Review.* November 2008 (product #R0811H).

Like the best-laid schemes of mice and men, the best-rehearsed speeches often go astray. No amount of preparation can counter an audience's perception that the speaker is calculating or insincere. Why do so many managers have trouble communicating authenticity to their listeners?

Morgan, a communications coach for more than two decades, offers advice for overcoming this difficulty. Recent brain research shows that natural, unstudied gestures—what Morgan calls the "second conversation"—express emotions or impulses a split second before our thought processes have turned them into words. So the timing of practiced gestures will always be subtly off, just enough to be picked up by listeners' unconscious ability to read body language.

If you can't practice the unspoken part of your delivery, what can you do? Tap into four basic impulses underlying your speech—to be open to the audience, to connect with it, to be passionate, and to "listen" to how the audience is responding—and then rehearse your presentation with each in mind. You can become more open, for instance, by imagining that you're speaking to your spouse or a close friend. To more readily connect, focus on needing to engage your listeners and then to keep their attention, as if you were speaking to a child who isn't heeding your words. To convey your passion, identify the feelings behind your speech and let them come through. To listen, think about what the audience is probably feeling when you step up to the podium and be alert to the nonverbal messages of its members. Internalizing these four impulses as you practice will help you come across as relaxed and authentic, and your body language will take care of itself.

Morgan, Nick. "The Kinesthetic Speaker: Putting Action into Words." *Harvard Business Review*. April 2001 (product #R0104G).

Speeches and presentations offer an interesting catch-22: Executives don't want to spend long hours creating them, and people don't want to sit for long hours listening to them. Ultimately, though, executives can't live without them. That's because a good speech or presentation has the power to inspire people to act on the speaker's behalf and create change.

Author Nick Morgan, a longtime speechwriter and speaking coach, says what's most often lacking in today's speeches and presentations is what he calls the "kinesthetic connection." Many good speakers connect aurally with their audiences, telling dramatic stories and effectively pacing their speeches to hold people's attention. Others connect visually, with a vivid film clip or a killer slide. Some people do both, but not many also connect kinesthetically. Morgan says the kinesthetic speaker feeds an audience's primal hunger to experience a presentation on a physical, as well as an intellectual, level. Through awareness of their own physical presence—gestures, posture, movements—and through the effective use of the space in which they present, kinesthetic speakers can create potent nonverbal messages that reinforce their verbal ones.

In this article, Morgan describes techniques for harnessing kinesthetic power and creating a sense of intimacy with an audience—a closeness that is more widely expected from speakers since the advent of television. For instance, kinesthetic speakers should make use of audience proxies—individuals in the crowd who serve as representatives for the others. Ultimately, the author says, a speech or presentation offers something of great value to business executives: It's the best vehicle for winning trust from large groups of people—be they employees, colleagues, or shareholders.

Tannen, Deborah. "The Power of Talk: Who Gets Heard and Why." *Harvard Business Review*. September 1995 (product #R9977).

Most managerial work happens through talk—discussions, meetings, presentations, negotiations. It is through talk that managers evaluate others and are themselves judged.

Using research carried out in a variety of workplace settings, linguist Deborah Tannen demonstrates how conversational style often overrides what we say, affecting who gets heard, who gets credit, and what gets done. Tannen's linguistic perspective provides managers with insight into why there is so much poor communication. Gender plays an important role. Tannen traces the ways in which women's styles can undermine them in the workplace, making them seem less competent, confident, and self-assured than they are. She analyzes the underlying social dynamic created through talk in common workplace interactions. She argues that a better understanding of linguistic style will make managers better listeners and more effective communicators, allowing them to develop more flexible approaches to a full range of managerial activities.

Sources

Primary sources for this book

Harvard Business School Publishing. Harvard Manage-Mentor. Boston: Harvard Business Publishing, 2002.

Harvard Business School Publishing. *Pocket Mentor: Giving Presentations*. Boston: Harvard Business School Press, 2007.

Other sources consulted

Duarte, Nancy. *HBR Guide to Persuasive Presentations*. Boston: Harvard Business Review Press, 2012.

Harvard Business School Publishing. *Harvard Business Essentials*: *Business Communication*. Boston: Harvard Business School Press, 2003.

Morrisey, George L., Thomas Sechrest, and Wendy B. Warman. *Loud and Clear: How to Prepare and Deliver Effective Business and Technical Presentations*. Reading, MA: Addison-Wesley Publishing Company, 1997.

Index

action, call to, 33
analogies, 61
anecdotes, 19. *See also* humor
arguments
  sequence for, 28–31, 33
  supporting, 27–28
assumptions, of audience,
  18–19, 52
attention, of audience, 20,
  29, 60–61
attire, 54
audience
  assumptions of, 18–19, 52
  engagement, 43, 60–61
  following up with, 81–82
  getting attention of, 20, 29
  input from, 32, 67–72
  interacting with, 55, 71–72
  knowing your, 17–21
  needs of, 21, 31
  nonverbal cues from, 60

questions from, 53, 62–63,
  67–72
relationship with, 19
size of, 17–18
surveying, 14, 61
test, 52

background information,
  18, 28
breathing, 54, 60

call to action, 33
clothing, 54
colleagues, feedback from,
  77–78
contact information, 71
conversational tone, 53, 59
core message, 26, 62
critiques, 75–78

Index

data, supporting, 27–28, 62–63
debriefing, 75–78
deliverables, 14, 20, 38, 71
delivery
  analyzing your, 75–78
  practicing your, 51–55
  tips for, 59–63

engagement, 43, 60–61
equipment, 39–40, 52
eye contact, 60

facial expression, 60
facts, 27–28
feedback, 38, 52, 68, 71, 77–78
flexibility, 61–63
follow-up, with audience, 71, 81–82

goals
  conflicts in attendees', 19
  defining, 11–14, 26

humor, 61. *See also* anecdotes

information, background, 18, 28
input, from audience, 32

jargon, 53

main point, defining, 26
mental preparation, 51, 54–55
message
  arguments and data to support, 27–28
  crafting your, 25–33
  defining core, 26
  organizing, 28–31, 33
metrics, of success, 14, 17

need, defining, 30–31
nervousness, 55, 59, 77
nonverbal cues, 60

objective, 11–12, 14, 17, 26
opening, 29–30, 76
organization, of presentation, 28–31, 33

outcomes, desired, 12–13, 14, 17

pace, 38, 59
performance analysis, 75–78
personal stories, 20, 61. *See also* story, use of
positive statements, 54
PowerPoint, 44, 45. *See also* slide presentations
preparation, 51–55
presentations
  audience input during, 32, 67–72
  crafting message for, 25–33
  debriefing following, 75–78
  delivery of, 59–63
  ending, 33
  flexibility during, 61–63
  follow-up, 71, 81–82
  goal for, 11–14, 26
  key to, 3
  length of, 30, 38–39
  mental preparation for, 51, 54–55
  openings, 29–30, 76
  organization of, 28–31, 33
  reasons for giving, 7–8, 11–14
  rehearsing, 51–54
  visual aids for, 40, 43–47
problem
  defining, 30–31
  solution for, 31
purpose, of presentation, 7–8, 11–14

questions, from audience, 53, 62–63, 67–72

rapport with audience, 19, 30
rehearsals, 51–54
relaxation techniques, 54, 60. *See also* stress reduction
resources
  for further information, 83–92
  identifying, 37–40

self-critique, 75–77
slide presentations, 44–47, 51, 76
solutions, 31

Index

sound system, 59
story, use of, 20, 29, 31, 61
stress reduction, 54, 60.
    See also relaxation
    techniques
success, measurement of,
    14, 17

technical difficulties, 62, 63,
    77
test audience, 52

time, for presentation, 30,
    38–39

venues, 37–38, 54
visual aids, 40, 43–47
    choosing appropriate, 44
    creating effective, 44–47
    uses of, 43–44, 53

wrap-up, 33

Notes

Smarter than the average guide.

Harvard Business Review Guides

If you enjoyed this book and want more comprehensive guidance on essential professional skills, turn to the **HBR Guides series**. Packed with concise, practical tips from leading experts—and examples that make them easy to apply—these books help you master big work challenges with advice from the most trusted brand in business.

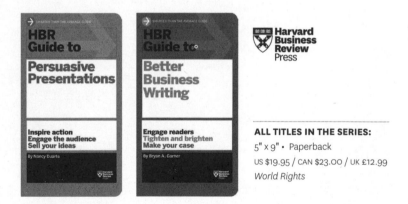

ALL TITLES IN THE SERIES:
5" x 9" • Paperback
US $19.95 / CAN $23.00 / UK £12.99
World Rights